The Book of
URBAN
LEGENDS

D0510741

The Book of
URBAN
LEGENDS

Robin Reeve

Michael O'Mara Humour

First published in Great Britain in 2002 by
Michael O'Mara Books Limited
9 Lion Yard
Tremadoc Road
London SW4 7NQ

Copyright © Michael O'Mara Books Ltd 2002

All rights reserved. No part of this publication may be
reproduced, stored in a retrieval system, or transmitted by
any means, without the prior permission in writing of the
publisher, nor be otherwise circulated in any form of
binding or cover other than that in which it is published
and without a similar condition including this condition
being imposed on the subsequent purchaser.

A CIP catalogue record for this book is available from the
British Library

ISBN 1-85479-932-0

3 5 7 9 10 8 6 4

Designed and typeset by Design 23

www.mombooks.com

Printed and bound in Great Britain by Cox & Wyman Ltd.,
Reading, Berkshire

Contents

Urban Legend:

A story, especially one with a shocking or amusing ending, related as having actually happened, usually to someone vaguely connected to the teller.

INTRODUCTION

One day, not so long ago, having just been told a extraordinary story about a friend of a friend, involving some Welsh sheep and some black jelly beans, I got to thinking about all the wonderful stories that I have heard over the years and how many more there must still be out there.

With that in mind, I decided to devote myself to seeking out people who have featured in one way or another in these unusual, funny and unlikely stories. I travelled extensively and met a wide range of people in a variety of countries and settings. The sometimes shocking tales I came across during my research are collected here in one volume. Some of them were told to me first-hand, others by friends or relatives of the heroes and heroines. I have also included a few pieces of local lore and legend from the countries I visited.

This unputdownable selection of weird and wonderful occurences is for all those who enjoy a good yarn, whether funny, fantastical or just plain spooky.

Pigs Might Fly: Animals

Don't you know there's a war on?

Vlad Blasikova, an imaginative soldier serving in the Russian army during World War II, had the bright idea of attaching mines to dogs and training them to run underneath enemy tanks. He explained his plan to his superiors who thought it an excellent scheme. To begin with, fifty dogs were trained up and in their practice exercises, the plan worked perfectly.

Unfortunately, when it came to the execution of the scheme, they found one, rather important, flaw. The Russians had only been able to use their own tanks to train the dogs with, which were diesel powered. When the dogs were taken to the battlefield, they refused to go under the German tanks because these were petrol driven. Instead, the dogs headed straight back to the Russian engines, and ended blowing up them instead.

Military Mayhem

World War II threw up a slightly more successful innovation, when the British trained seagulls to fly over enemy U-boats and poo on their periscopes.

In the United States, bears have been used by the US Air Force to test the efficiency of ejector seats.

Came down in the last shower?

Miguel, a Mexican student whose girlfriend Conchita lived over a hundred miles away, drove every Friday night to visit her for the weekend. One Friday night he had a very lucky escape as his journey was considerably more eventful than the others. Miguel told his girlfriend that he had had to stop several miles short of his destination to change a flat tyre. Ahead of him a tornado had sucked a load of toads from a nearby lake and dropped them on to a motorway. All the squashed toads made the road really slippery and caused an eighteen-car pile up.

Dangerous Cargo

While making a routine refuelling stop the crew of a Russian cargo plane spotted a cow grazing just off the runway. Keen to make a little extra money from their trip, they decided to steal the animal. They stashed it in the cargo hold, but the cow became very frightened when the plane took off, and she began to charge about. The worried crew decided that it was too dangerous to keep the animal on board, and duly threw it out of the hold. Even out of the plane, however, the cow still managed to create chaos and destruction – it landed on a Japanese fishing trawler and sunk it instantly.

Like it or Lump it

Carol, a student from Manchester University, had taken a gap year during her years of study. Shortly after returning from a trip round the world, she noticed a small lump on her neck. Over the next few weeks the lump steadily grew, until she decided to see a doctor. The doctor was unable to diagnose the lump, but since it did not seem to be affecting her health in any other way, he assumed it was harmless and sent her away. Some time later, when Carol had all but forgotten about it, the lump suddenly broke and hundreds of tiny spiders spilled out. Horrified, the girl returned to the doctor who consulted his medical books and found details of a very rare breed of South American spider which likes to lay its eggs on the flesh of mammals. It was this that Carol had had the misfortune to encounter while in South America.

A Lot Of Hot Air?

A woman in Kansas was carefully preparing her prize poodle for an important show. She had washed it, combed it and was about to blowdry it when her hairdryer fused at the last minute. Priding herself on her resourcefulness, the woman came up with the idea of putting the dog in the microwave in order to dry its fur in time for the show. She got a nasty shock when the dog exploded.

A Fishy Business

A group of fishermen were in a bar, morosely drowning their sorrows after a particularly disastrous fishing trip. That day, the men had not had much luck and so had been particularly pleased when, on their way back to shore, they caught a large shoal of herring. However, they hadn't reckoned on having such a huge catch on their hands. When they tried to reel it in, the herring all dived for the sea bottom at the same time, and their combined weight managed not only to break the crane, but also to capsize their boat.

Flippering Cheek!

Dutch researchers in the Arctic region lost a valuable source of funding when one of their sponsors, an elderly billionaire, passed away, leaving his entire fortune to a local dogs' home. Forced to make financial cutbacks, they eventually found a much cheaper and more effective way of tracking seals. Instead of using radar collars, they have been gluing coned-shaped party hats with numbers on them to the seals' heads.

The Biter Bit

Mr Andrews was walking in Queensland, Australia when he passed a teenager fishing in a lake. Stopping to make small talk, Mr Andrews asked if he had caught much. The teenager told him he had caught quite a few fish, but that the worms he had found to use as bait kept biting him. Thinking this rather strange, Mr Andrews took a look at the worms in the bait box and saw that they were, in fact, tiny, but deadly poisonous, snakes. The man immediately took the fisherman, who had almost thirty bites on his hands, to hospital where he fell into a coma. The teenager almost died, but in the end made a full recovery. Now, when the victim goes on a fishing trip, he buys his bait from a shop.

A Case Of Mistaken Identity

A couple on holiday in Bali returned to their hotel room one night to find a stray cat sitting on their window ledge. The cat was a little bedraggled and thin, so, being cat-lovers, the couple cleaned it up and fed it. The cat obviously took a liking to them and stayed with them for the remainder of their visit. When the time came for the pair to return home, they had grown so fond of it that they made arrangements for it to be shipped back to America with them, thinking it would make an ideal companion for the poodle they already had.

On the first day they left it alone in the house. To their horror, however, they returned to find that their beloved poodle had been attacked and the cat was busy eating its remains. It turned out that the 'cat' had, in fact, been an overgrown water rat, a fairly common species in Bali.

Ring Any Bells?

Mrs Jones from Leicester, thrilled at the news that her daughter, who had been living in Australia for the last eleven years, was finally returning to England permanently, decided to buy her a mobile phone for Christmas, so that they could keep in close contact. However, on Christmas Day, when the time came to open the presents, all she could find beneath the tree was a torn open, empty box. Mr Jones suggested that she call the phone, which she duly did – whereupon a distinct ringing sound was heard coming from the family's pet dog.

Chinese Whispers

A Chinese family were seeking to do a house-swap with an English family and advertized in the London press. Their only requirement was that the English house should have a duck pond. The Robinsons from Wiltshire responded and an arrangement was reached whereby each family would spend two weeks in one another's homes, enabling them to enjoy a relatively cheap holiday abroad. The Robinsons had a lovely time, staying in a beautiful house in a pretty Beijing suburb, and came home delighted with the experience. However, when they returned to their house, they found that their ducks had been shot and eaten. They were not keen to repeat the swap the following year.

Cat-astrophe Or Feline Fable?

Firemen in Shropshire were called out to rescue a cat from a tree. After the successful rescue, they should perhaps have left well alone, but the old woman who owned the cat was so grateful that she invited them all back for tea. After a cuppa and a few biscuits, the firemen climbed back into their fire engine and, waving genially at the old woman, began to reverse out of the driveway. Regrettably, the driver failed to check in his rearview mirror and ran over the cat that they had gone to so much trouble to rescue earlier.

Drunk As A Bird?

People living in a suburban street in Nottingham were surprised to see over a dozen robins lying semi-conscious on the pavement. From the red stains around their beaks, experts deduced that they must have eaten partly fermented berries from the nearby bushes. This had been enough to render the small birds very drunk!

For The Birds?

The sky over a penguin colony in the Falklands has been made a no-fly zone after it was discovered that the penguins were falling on to their backs while trying to watch planes overhead. Once toppled, the flightless birds are unable to get up again.

Light My Fire?

An elderly lady in Edinburgh asked her granddaughter to look after her pet budgie while she was away on holiday in the Canary Islands. However, the day before she was due back, the granddaughter's boyfriend came round and, taking pity on the caged bird, decided to let it have a fly around the room. The budgie was so excited to have a little more freedom that it flew out of the cage and straight into a window, breaking its leg. Knowing how fond his girlfriend and her grandmother were of the bird, the boy was panic-stricken, but eventually hit upon the idea of tying a match to the bird's leg as a splint. Very pleased with his ingenuity, he put it back in its cage and left. However, what the boyfriend had not realized was that the cage was lined with sandpaper. As the budgie dragged itself across the cage floor, the match ignited and the unfortunate bird caught fire. All that was left to greet the grandmother on her return was a pile of ashes!

Bird-Brained

Birds are a major cause of plane crashes, often cracking the glass in cockpit windows in mid-flight. To help test the strength of the glass, the US Air Force developed a gun that fired dead chickens at the glass at speed. The French government borrowed the idea to test the glass in their high-speed trains. However, when they fired their gun, the chicken not only smashed the train windows but also took out the driver's head-rest and embedded itself in the rear wall of the driver's cab. At a loss to know why the experiment had gone so wrong, the French sent their test results to the US. The US officials sent a one-line reply back: 'Next time, defrost the chickens.'

Did You Know?

Researchers have found that when chickens watch television they lay twenty per cent more eggs.

What a Gull!

A teenage boy in Cumbria was a keen footballer, though he was no David Beckham. During a charity football match, in the dying seconds of the game, he volleyed the ball from the other end of the pitch in a desperate last-ditch attempt to score. The ball was going way off-course and all hope looked lost, when suddenly a seagull swooped down and inadvertently headed it into the net. The seagull flew off unharmed, and the goal was allowed – the boy's first and only goal of the season!

Box of Surprises

A woman in New Mexico had a surprise when she bought a large box of chicken nuggets from a fast-food restaurant. She sat down to enjoy her meal, but when she opened the box she found a chicken's head, complete with its beak, crown and a few feathers. In compensation, the restaurant gave her a free box of nuggets.

Crocodile Tears?

A young man was sitting on the lavatory in his basement apartment in New York when he suddenly felt a searing pain in his left buttock. He leapt up from the loo and found a baby alligator attached by its teeth to his behind. He headed straight to the hospital to have a tetanus shot where the doctor who treated him was able to explain what had happened, as he had treated other such cases. The appearance of the exotic creature in a toilet was a manifestation of the recent New York trend of yuppies adopting the baby reptiles as pets. However, many owners had second thoughts when the alligators began to grow, and had flushed them down the toilet. Against all the odds, the alligators had managed to thrive and multiply in the sewers beneath the city. Visitors in New York are advised to look carefully into the toilet bowl before sitting down!

Resurrected Rabbit

One morning, as was his usual habit, a man in North London let his dog out into the garden to have a run about before breakfast. This morning, however, when the dog returned, it had the muddy remains of a white rabbit in its mouth. To his horror, the man recognized it as the rabbit belonging to the family next door. The man knew that the incident would do little for neighbourly harmony and, feeling guilty, decided to cover it up. He prised the dead bunny from the dog's mouth, took it indoors, washed it thoroughly and, finally, carefully blow-dried it. He sneaked next door and replaced the restored rabbit back in its hutch, hoping that his neighbours would be none the wiser.

When the family returned and discovered their dead pet the man heard their cries of grief and surprise. He came out in the garden and pretended to be just as surprised as they were.

'What a terrible shock for you,' he told the mother.

'Yes, isn't it?' agreed the woman. 'Especially since it died last night and I buried it in the garden before leaving for work this morning!'

Did You Know?

American moose get so lonely during the mating season that they attempt courtship with dairy cows and inanimate objects.

A Swedish navy boat pursued a group of minke whales for several months, believing them to be foreign submarines violating Swedish water.

A small Cantonese province in southern China is well known for its people's strange appetites. They will eat anything – dead or alive. In the market you can find tigers' paws, bears, cats, decomposing monkeys, mongoose parts, owls, doves and deer penises.

Here Kitty Kitty...

A young woman in Edinburgh was most distressed to find that her new kitten had managed to get itself stuck up a willow tree in the garden. After several hours of trying to coax it down with threats, pleas and morsels of fish, she called the fire

brigade to help. When they arrived they decided that not only were the tree's branches too fragile to support the ladder, but that the ladder was also too short for the firemen to be able to reach the cat. After thinking a while, they came up with an idea to overcome both these hurdles. Two men held the ladder while a third man climbed up it far enough to throw a loop of rope around the branch holding the kitten. The idea was that the man would then gently pull the branch close enough for him to grab the cat.

Unfortunately, at the crucial moment, one of the men holding the ladder below was stung by a large wasp, causing him to temporarily loosen his grip. With the ladder swaying erratically, the fireman holding the rope accidentally pulled it a little hard before letting go in order to keep his balance on the ladder. The cat was seen flying at a rate of knots in the direction of Glasgow...

All was not lost, however, for a couple of blocks away, a couple out enjoying the sun in their garden were shocked and amazed to see a small kitten come hurtling out of the sky and land safely in their empty paddling pool!

A Leap
Of Faith:
Religion

Clerical Clangers...

A schoolboy was surprised to receive a letter from his Romanian penfriend detailing an unusual scandal that had broken out in his small, usually sedate, rural village. The vicar there had just been put on trial for seducing vulnerable married women. One of his ruses had been to tell them that their husbands had confessed to cheating on them, before he offered the distraught wives some bodily comfort in his confession box.

Surprise Surprise!

There was a pope in the ninth century who was actually a woman. Her disguise was only rumbled when she became pregnant!

True Believer

A couple in Texas, who were both atheists, had not been getting along. One night they were fighting badly and ended up shooting each other. Their orphaned young daughter was taken into care and happened to be placed with foster parents who were deeply religious. The foster mother took the little girl to Sunday school for the first time and, during the session, the Sunday school teacher held up a picture of Jesus and asked, 'Does anyone know this man?' The little girl stood up and replied, 'Yes, he was the one holding me when my parents killed each other.'

Saints alive!

A nun in Santiago has the ability to turn herself into a bun.

A group known as the Second Coming Project are seeking to clone Jesus from DNA taken from holy relics.

A rabbi in Boston, America, made an unusual satellite broadcast to his followers. He declared it to be acceptable to pick your nose on the Sabbath, despite the risk of pulling out nasal hair (the cutting of hair is forbidden on the Sabbath).

A religious fanatic in Michigan was hit by a truck while crossing a road. He was carrying a banner proclaiming: 'The end of the world is nigh.'

It's a miracle!

A boy in Luton was sitting out on his parents' front porch, writing an essay on why he didn't believe in God when he was struck by lightning.

A heavy drinker from Manchester bought a packet of pork scratchings from a pub, and was amazed to find a scratching shaped like the Virgin Mary holding the baby Jesus. The scratching was donated to a museum and the man gave up alcohol and became a born-again Christian.

After her baptism, an eight-year-old girl slipped over and cut her knee. A piece of sticking plaster was applied to the wound and, when it was removed, the blood-stained plaster was found to show the image of Christ. The girl's father reproduced the image and sold it for two dollars a copy.

Water Change of Heart

A young atheist training to dive in the Olympic Games turned up at his local pool in Aberdeen to practise one night, only to find that all the lights were out. Nevertheless, he decided that there was enough moonlight for him to dive in the pool. Thus, he climbed to the top of the highest board and prepared his dive. He went to the end of the board and extended his arms out, when suddenly he caught sight of his shadow on the far wall. What he saw was a giant crucifix lit by the moon. The man was so moved that instead of diving he knelt down to pray. At that moment the janitor walked in and switched on the lights, only to reveal that the pool had been drained for repairs.

A Purely Academic Argument

An intimidating philosophy professor at an American university was a confirmed atheist and did his best to convert his students to his point of view. At the end of every semester, for the previous twenty years, he had asked if any of his students still believed in God. The students were all too afraid of being ridiculed to raise a hand and admit that they did. He would then say: 'If God does exist then surely he could stop this chalk from breaking.' At that point, he would drop his chalk and it would shatter on the ground. This continued until finally, one year, a particularly opinionated student was brave enough to admit that he did believe in God. Both the students and the professor looked at the outspoken young man in amazement. 'Well then,' said the professor, 'show me that he can stop this chalk from breaking, and I'll believe in God, too'; whereupon he dropped the piece of chalk. However, it fell into a crease on his shirt, rolled gently down his trouser leg, over his shoe and on to the ground intact. To everyone's embarrassment, the middle-aged professor burst into tears and fled from the lecture theatre. The student, meanwhile, got up and spent the remaining hour of the lesson giving a lecture on the existence of God.

Did you Know...?

There is a religion for people who don't care about religion.

The Hubble telescope has discovered an image of Jesus in space.

Bible experts recently deciphered a complex code in the holy book with the aid of computers. They discovered that the beginning of Armageddon will be around the year 2005.

If you log on to www.prayer-o-matic.com you will get an instant reply from God.

Heaven forbid...

Some Americans worship at the following churches: The Church of Shatnerology (dedicated to William Shatner – alias Star Trek's Captain Kirk), the Church of Buscemi (dedicated to the actor Steve Buscemi), the First Church of Presleytarian (Elvis), the Church of the Gerbil, the Church of the Dead Cow, the Church of the Avocado, the Church of the Holy Pear, the Church of the Burnt Onion Ring, the Church of the Spinning Hamster, the Church of the Twinkie and the Church of the Profit.

If over 25,000 people wrote down 'Jedi Knight' as their religion in a census, it would force the government to grant it official status.

Dead
or a Liar:
Bizarre
Deaths

Rough Justice?

Officials in Malaysia have recently been reconsidering the death penalty. Three executioners have died in the last three years – all of them met their end while posing for tourist photos with their heads in a noose.

He's Toast

During a speech at the Toast Appreciators' Club in Johannesburg, Danny Detroit said: 'Appreciate life while you can because death could strike at any moment–'

To punctuate his speech he took a big bite out of a piece of toast; unfortunately, it got stuck in his throat and he choked to death.

Unkind Fates

A man was killed when he got out of his car to watch a passing tornado and a cow that had been sucked up by the whirling air landed on him.

A man in Mexico was stabbed to death by dry spaghetti during a hurricane.

Helmut, a Hungarian chicken-thief, was forced by an angry mob to eat live chickens until he died.

A Canadian man called 'North' was killed when, during a severe gale, a weather vane blew off a nearby church and impaled him.

Not Such A Good Idea?

In order to settle a family argument two brothers from Bombay were told to hold their breath under water. The one who held it the longest would win. Both men drowned.

John Forrester, a well-known practical joker from Devon, sucked a pea up his nose while showing off to friends. He then tried to remove it by wiggling a pen up his nostril. Unfortunately, his mother came to see what all the laughter was about and, as she pushed open the door, she caught the end of the pen, driving it into her son's brain and killing him instantly.

A young man from New Jersey on an acid trip believed he was an orange and peeled himself.

Warning – Animals Are Dangerous!

The smallest man in the Circus, named Odin, was swallowed by a hippo while he was checking its teeth.

A man in southern China tried to subdue an angry snake by placing the butt of his gun on the snake's neck. However, the snake coiled its tail around the trigger and shot the man in the head.

In South Africa a man was killed by an angry elephant. He had tried to milk it after a friend told him this was how to attain the most powerful aphrodisiac in the world.

Driven To Distraction...

A woman driver was applying her lipstick when a van suddenly pulled out in front of her, forcing her to brake sharply. She swallowed the lipstick and choked to death.

Three teenagers stole a jeep in order to joyride. While driving down the road, the driver tried to show off to some passing girls by pulling out the keys and yelling, 'Look, no keys.' However, the steering lock engaged, whereupon the jeep drove in a straight line into a petrol pump and exploded.

A Russian farmer was found frozen to death with his lips stuck to the lock of his car. Apparently he had tried to defrost the lock by blowing on it, whereupon his lips had stuck to the freezing metal.

Some of us Twigged...

A man who was climbing a tree to collect mangoes was shot by hunters, who later claimed they mistook him for a squirrel.

A scuba diver was found at the top of a charred tree amid the remains of a forest fire. Apparently fire-planes sent to tackle the blaze had sucked up the hapless diver when they swooped down to draw water from a lake. He was then dropped, along with several tons of water, on to the flames!

It's Just Hearsay

A deaf man in Los Angeles was shot dead while talking to his friend in sign language. A passing gang thought he was using rival gang signals.

That Sinking Feeling...

A man was halfway through drinking a bottle of cola when he started to notice a strange taste. He emptied the rest of the bottle in the sink, only to find a dead rat at the bottom of it – whereupon the man had a heart attack and died.

Left In The Dark

One Saturday night in the middle of winter, a young sophomore staying in halls at an American university went out to a party with her boyfriend. She said goodbye to her roommate, who had been ill for several days and was therefore staying in that night. As soon as the girl reached the party, she realised that she had forgotten her purse and so had to return to her campus hall to retrieve it. Her roommate had already switched off the lights and gone to bed by the time the girl returned. Not wishing to disturb the roommate, the girl did not switch the lights on but fumbled around in the dark to find her purse. She could hear heavy breathing in the dark, which she assumed to be her roommate, still suffering from the aftereffects of a heavy cold. Once she found the purse, she quietly closed the door behind her and headed back to the party.

That night, she didn't return to her room, staying instead with a friend. However, when she did return in the morning it was to find the room cordoned off by the police and surrounded by shocked students. The girl's roommate had been brutally stabbed at some point during the night. The girl was able to help the police pinpoint exactly when it happened when she saw the chilling message written in red lipstick on the mirror in the room: 'LUCKY FOR YOU THAT YOU DIDN'T TURN THE LIGHTS ON, OR IT WOULD HAVE BEEN YOU AS WELL!'

A Ghost of a Chance: Strange Hauntings

Taken For A Ride...

About ten years ago, in the heart of Somerset, a man and his wife were driving home from their weekly shop. They came to a crossroads and stopped at the junction, whereupon the woman spotted a girl on the opposite side of the road signalling for a lift. The couple felt sorry for her because of the heavy rain and her young age, and so offered her a ride home. She told them her address and they set off. The three of them chatted all the way to the girl's house, but when they arrived and the couple turned to say goodbye, the girl had suddenly vanished. Concerned for her well-being, they went to the front door of the address she had given. A woman answered and the couple explained what had just happened. The woman then told them: 'My daughter was killed at that same crossroads ten years ago today, she was struck by a car while trying to hitch a lift home.'

You've Been Framed

Eagle-eyed filmgoers have spotted that, in the film *Three Men and a Baby*, in the scene where Ted Danson is talking to the mother of the baby in the apartment that the men share, it is possible to see the figure of a little boy. Having looked into the history of the apartment used for filming, two cameramen who had worked on the film discovered that a boy committed suicide in the apartment one year before the film was shot. He had shot himself, and, if you watch the scene very carefully, you can see that he appears to be holding a gun upside down.

Knock Me Down...

An architect was staying with an elderly couple while working on some plans for renovating their country manor. After supper the man excused himself in order to use the bathroom. On his way back to the dining room, he met a little girl, wearing an old-fashioned, white nightgown. She looked extremely upset, so the architect tried to console her. However, she refused to speak to him, and eventually he told her that he would go and look for her parents, believing them to be servants in the house. But at this the child looked even more scared and grasped the man by the wrist. Thinking that she was worried that he would not come back, he gave her his watch to keep until he returned.

Naturally, the architect asked his hosts where he could find the child's parents. However, the elderly couple looked horrified, and the woman became very angry, saying: 'Is this some kind of joke? There is no one else in this house but the three of us. The servants went home hours ago.'

The architect demanded that they come

with him to see the child for themselves, but she had disappeared. The next day the architect returned home. Nothing else was said about the little girl, although the couple decided not to go ahead with the renovations.

Ten years later the couple died and it was decided that the manor house should be pulled down. The same architect was called in to design apartment blocks on the site. Demolition of the house was underway, when the architect received a call from a panicked worker. When he arrived at the site he found that they had uncovered a concealed room in which lay the skeleton of a child, dressed in a white nightgown, and wearing a man's wristwatch.

Bear-Faced Cheek...

A young man was asked to housesit in Dorset for a family friend. Before taking on the task he was warned that the house was haunted by a friendly ghost. The owners told him that the ghost had a favourite teddy bear and would sometimes make a lot of noise if the bear got mislaid. Highly amused by this, on his first night at the house, the man invited several of his friends over for a haunted-house party. However, much to everyone's disappointment, the night passed uneventfully.

The next night he spent alone. At around eleven o'clock he went to bed and fell asleep. However, in the middle of the night he was woken up by the sound of a stereo playing. Perplexed, he went to investigate. He found the room where the music was coming from, but as he went inside the stereo switched itself off. Slightly bemused, but being very tired from the night before, he shut the door and started to return to bed. However, the music started up again. He opened the door for the second time, but as he did so the stereo again switched itself off. He closed the door again and this time the music immediately came back on. For the third time he opened the door and this time the stereo stayed on. He walked to the end of the room and switched off the stereo at the plug socket. The room fell silent and he turned to leave. It was then that he saw the teddy bear sitting in the doorway.

On Further Examination...

Two boys from London had recently finished their GCSE examinations and were awaiting their results. One night they decided to use a ouija board, hoping to get a sneak preview of their grades. After an hour of trying they eventually contacted the spirit of a man who had recently died in a freak boating accident. The spirit gave them their grades for each exam and the two boys wrote them down.

The next day the boys told their friends about what they had done and of the predictions. When the results finally came through, they had both got exactly the same results as those the ghost had given them.

Heads And Tales...

There have been numerous sightings of a headless motorcyclist riding around the country lanes near Penzance. The story goes that a biker became stuck behind a builder's lorry. The lorry had to brake suddenly because of a stray sheep in the road. This sudden braking caused a metal pipe to slide out of the back of the lorry and decapitate the motorcyclist. To this day, the man still rides the route home on the anniversary of his death.

A Spirited Story

In the 1960s, a pupil called the school chaplain to his room. Apparently, over a period of a few months, things had started to move around by themselves. By the time the priest came, books were flying about, the desk lamp was switching on and off and pens were scribbling words all over the walls. Although terrified, the priest began to read from the Bible in order to drive the evil spirits away. After half an hour, the lights suddenly exploded in their sockets and all went still. The room was then sealed shut and the boy, emotionally disturbed by his experience, left the school. The room is still boarded up to this day.

Seeing Visions

In some villages in remote parts of South America it is believed that if you look through the keyhole of a church at midnight on New Year's Eve you will see visions of those who will die in the coming year.

Keeping Track?

In the early 1920s, a group of children were killed at a railway crossing. They had been playing on the line and had gone to the aid of a friend who had fallen and become trapped. Despite their best efforts, they had been unable to stop an oncoming train, and all of them had been crushed by its wheels.

Nearly seventy years later, a school bus stalled on the same crossing and the driver was unable to restart it. Panic-stricken, he heard the sound of a train bearing down upon them. He repeatedly tried the ignition but to no avail. He was just about to order the children off the bus when, mysteriously, it began to move forwards. The bus cleared the line just in time and the train roared by them.

Totally nonplussed, the driver turned to the children to check that they were okay. The children at the back of the bus told him that a group of young children in old-fashioned clothes had pushed the bus clear, but that they had vanished as soon as the train went past.

Queer as Folk: People Problems

Spaced Out?

Everyone has heard about Neil Armstrong's famous line upon first setting foot on the moon. More cryptic, however, were his words on leaving it – 'Good luck, Mr Gorsky'. It was only after twenty-six years, and a great deal of speculation, that Mr Armstrong finally explained. He said that, when he was eleven, he had overheard his next door neighbour, Mrs Gorsky, shouting at her husband: 'Oral sex! You want oral sex! You'll get oral sex when that kid next door walks on the moon!'

Money Makes The Rumours Go Round

A woman in Blackpool was observed stuffing thousands of pounds into letter boxes, through car windows and into the hands of passers-by. When questioned, she said that she had won six million pounds on the lottery and was giving it away because nobody loved her.

Tyred Excuse

Two Canadian students on a skiing holiday in the Rockies were having such a good time that they decided to stay on for another couple of days. This meant that they missed their maths examination which was scheduled for the last day of the extended break. When they returned they told their professor that they had missed the exam because they had had a flat tyre, and asked for the test to be rescheduled. The professor agreed on the condition that they sit it in separate rooms.

When the time came to sit the exam, both students found the first few pages, which were only worth a few points, very easy. However, when they turned to the last page, there was only one question, worth ninety per cent of the total mark: 'Which tyre?'

Testing Times

A student in one of the most prestigious of the British universities had enjoyed far too good a time partying during his final year to get down to work on his dissertation. He had the idea, supposedly foolproof, of visiting a university far away in Scotland, and copying one of the dissertations available in its library. Unfortunately, he failed to check the name of the person who had written it and was promptly expelled when his tutor recognized it to be his very own dissertation, written several years earlier when he was an undergraduate himself!

A Little Bit Backward?

Another student writing his dissertation had similarly spent far too much time in the student bar and not enough in the library. Having left it till the last minute he stayed up every night for five days, drinking copious amounts of coffee and coca cola and taking large quantities of speed, to enable him to finish off his essay in time. He handed it in just within the deadline but had not had a chance to read it through. He therefore did not notice that in his frantic, drug-addled state he had written the entire thing backwards! The story did have a happy ending though, in that his university came to the conclusion that he must be dyslexic and allowed him another chance to complete it.

Missing Something?

Richey Edwards, the missing member of the Manic Street Preachers, has been found to be alive and living on a remote island off India.

Racked With Guilt?

A pair of Moldovan cousins living in the Ukraine and too poor to afford a funeral for their dead grandmother, rolled up her corpse in a rug and strapped it to their roof rack, to be taken back to Moldova for a cheaper burial.

When they stopped off for a meal, however, thieves made off with the car, still with the cousins' grandma attached.

And On That Note

A man who had been shopping in his local supermarket returned to his car to find that someone had crashed into it and badly damaged it. Furious at first, he was appeased when he spotted a note tucked into the windshield, thinking it would obviously contain an apology and the details of the person who had crashed into his car. However, when he read the note he found that it simply said: 'The people watching me think I am leaving my name and address but I'm NOT.'

Revenge Is Sweet...

A worker who had worked hard for many years in a sweet factory in a seaside town was unexpectedly made redundant. Very angry and bitter at being treated so badly by the company he had worked so long and hard for, he wanted revenge. Before leaving, he prepared a mile of sweet rock which should have read 'A Present From Blackpool' all the way through it. Instead, the hundreds of sticks of rock that ended up in the shops and kiosks read 'F**k off!'

Medical Misfits

A man attended a business meeting in a Moscow restaurant. Arriving early, he had a couple of drinks at the bar. The next thing he was aware of was waking up in a hotel bath. Various tubes were attached to his body and the hotel phone was on a chair within reach of his hand. When help arrived, it was found that the man's kidneys had been removed.

A woman in Vietnam was left in a MRI scanning tunnel for three days when the doctor performing the procedure forgot she was in there and went on holiday.

A two-year-old boy living in London has been dubbed 'termite boy' because he keeps eating wood. Doctors say it will not hurt him, unless the wood is painted or treated with chemicals.

Major Malfunction

During the height of the Cold War, a Russian officer noticed that the computer he was monitoring was flashing a warning of an impending nuclear attack. According to the computer, there were fifteen minutes before impact. However, suspecting that the ageing cosmos satellite, which was relaying information to the computer, was malfunctioning, the soldier decided to wait the fifteen minutes out rather than launching a counter strike which would have undoubtedly led to a full-blown nuclear war. Luckily he was right. Nevertheless, the stress of the event proved so much that he was sent to a mental hospital.

Après-Ski
Embarrassment

A woman on a skiing holiday in Austria was a complete novice, having only had a couple of dry-slope lessons. Nevertheless, her husband, an advanced skier, persuaded her, against her better judgement, to come on the slopes with him and his friends. She spent much of the day falling over and struggling to keep up with the group. The final insult was to find that her husband and the others had finished their lunch at the bar before she had even got there. Needing to go to the toilet but unwilling to lag even further behind, she nipped behind a tree and started to remove her ski-suit. However, in the process she lost her balance and her skis started to move forwards with her skisuit and underwear still round her ankles. After shooting off some distance down the slope, she eventually managed to stop herself and put her clothes back on. To her relief, the incident seemed to have gone largely unnoticed by anyone around.

Later that same evening, she was enjoying a well-deserved drink at the resort bar and started chatting to a man sitting by the bar who had his leg in plaster. In answer to her enquiry, the man told her how he had got his injury:

'You probably won't believe this,' he said. 'But I was sitting on a chairlift yesterday morning. I was about to get off, so I had lifted up the safety bar. Just then a half-naked woman shot by with her ski-suit around her ankles. I was so busy gawping that I fell out of the chair. Hence the broken leg.'

Write These Ones Off

A man in Canada went out drinking one night and had one too many shandies. Despite his intoxication he decided to drive home. He was stopped by two police officers who had noticed his car weaving erratically. They asked him to get out of his car so that they could administer a breathalyzer test. Just as he was about to take the test, the policemen were distracted by something happening a couple of blocks down the street, and the driver, seizing the opportunity to make his escape, quickly hopped back in the car and drove off. Despite still being very drunk, he made it home safely, congratulating himself on a close shave.

The next morning, he was awoken by the doorbell. Very hungover, he made his way downstairs to find the same two officers on his doorstep. They accused him of having being drunk and in charge of a vehicle the previous night, which he strenuously denied. His denials were somewhat undermined, however, when the officers opened up his garage to find their patrol car parked inside!

Double Trouble

Twins, John and Luke, aged eighteen and from Cumbria, both passed their driving test at the same time. They were both given identical cars as birthday presents from their mother. On the way home they each took separate routes and, at exactly the same time, slipped off the road and hit a tree. The twins were unhurt, but both cars were written off.

Late Licencing

A woman was trying to pass her driving test so that she could surprise her ageing parents, whom she hadn't seen in years. However, she failed the test thirty-six times. Finally she was successful and gained a licence. She drove the 150 miles to her parents' house only to find that they had both died that day.

You What!

In an insurance claim filed in Kentucky, a man explained that his car accident had occurred when he had, as he said, 'driven into the wrong house and hit a tree he didn't have'.

Smooth Criminal

A man's car with his wallet still in it was stolen from a car park in the US. Devastated, he took a taxi home only to find his car parked in his own driveway. Inside was a note apologizing for borrowing his car, explaining it to have been a medical emergency, and four tickets to the upcoming Mets baseball game by way of compensation.

Being huge Mets fans, he and his family were delighted by the tickets as well as the return of the car, and went to the game that Saturday. However, when they returned they found they had been robbed and their house all but emptied. The car 'borrower' had planned it all along – he had taken the man's home address, and keys, and, guessing that the man was a baseball fan from his Mets bumper sticker, had used the tickets as a way of getting him out of the house. Photos in the man's wallet had shown the robber that he had two sons and would therefore need four tickets to ensure the house would be entirely empty.

Food For Thought...

A man is suing a supermarket for offering too many irresistible bargains. He claims that he injured his back carrying the surplus products home.

A robber in Detroit tried to rob a supermarket by climbing through a skylight on top of the building. However, he found that the window was too small for him to get through. In an attempt to make himself thinner, he took off all his clothes and dropped them through the opening. He then tried again and managed to lower himself halfway through. Unfortunately, he then got stuck and had to call for help. The night watchman was somewhat surprised to find half a naked man dangling from the ceiling.

A woman in Manchester held up a store clerk with a plastic gun, crying: 'Carry my shopping home or I'll shoot you.' The clerk thus pushed the women's trolley the two miles back to her house with the woman walking behind him.

Indian muggers have been using snakes as hold-up weapons. They have been holding shopkeepers at snake-point while demanding money.

A Shot In The Dark

A middle-aged woman from Minnesota was on her way to visit her in-laws, when she decided to stop for some groceries. She bought some things and got back in her car, where several people observed her sitting holding the back of her head and looking panic-stricken. The store manager eventually came out and asked if she was all right. She said that she had been shot in the back off the head and that she was holding her brains in. An ambulance and the police were called. She was eventually persuaded to let go of the back of her head and, as she did so, a large slab of dough was seen to be stuck to her hair. It transpired that a tin of ready-to-bake dough that she had bought had been sitting close to the shop window and had warmed up. The heat of her car had been all that was needed for the expanding dough to explode out of its tin. The noise had sounded like a gun going off.

By The Book

When he discovered it was still one of the rules written in the university rule book an Oxford student demanded cakes and ale to accompany his exam. In revenge, the examiner, who was also familiar with the rule book, fined him five pounds for not wearing his sword to the exam – another of the archaic rules.

Not So Romantic Fiction

An Austrian man had been making harassing telephone calls of an extremely explicit sexual nature for over three years. One of his victims had obviously become very fed up with the caller and one day decided to leave the following message on her answer phone: 'I'm not in mood today. Please leave your number and I'll call you back tomorrow.' Foolishly, the man left both a dirty message and his number. He was arrested shortly afterwards.

A young hairdresser was on her own in the salon when a plump and sweaty man wearing a mac rushed in and asked for a quick trim. Despite being slightly wary of the stranger, the woman agreed and began to cut his hair. As she was doing so, she noticed the man's hands moving quickly back and forth under the robe she had given him to protect his clothes from the cut hair. She grabbed a large hairdryer and smacked him on the back of the head, rendering him unconscious. She then called the police who arrived promptly and asked her why she had attacked the man. She explained and demanded that they arrest the man when he came to. The officer pulled off the robe to check what the man had been doing under there. He turned to the hairdresser with a grin and explained that there was no law against cleaning your spectacles.

A woman in Bath was furious to find that her longterm lover had been seeing someone else on the side for many years. She immediately decided to leave him, but as a parting shot, she sewed shrimp into the seams of his curtains, turned up the thermostat and left him a note to say she would not be coming back. It took him weeks of living with the foul smell and frantically turning his house upside down before he discovered where the awful smell was coming from.

A man in Illinois decided to visit a strip club with a few friends to celebrate his stag night. He got a little more than he bargained for, however, when, having paid for a close-up lap dance, he was hit in the head by one of the dancer's breasts. He then tried to sue the strip club for having not only sustained whiplash and a slight concussion from the incident, but also for the emotional stress he had had to undergo when he explained the cause of his injury to his bride-to-be.

A teenage boy finally plucked up the courage to ask out a girl he had been keen on for a long while. Not wanting to seem ill-prepared or – god forbid, unwilling – should the occasion to have sex by any chance arise, he stopped off at a chemist to buy some condoms. It being his first time, he was very embarrassed to ask for them and in his attempts to seem grown-up he quipped to the pharmacist about how he was expecting to 'get lucky tonight'. The pharmacist nodded knowingly. To the boy's horror, when he drove round later that day to pick up his date for the evening the door was opened by the girl's father – the very same pharmacist who had served him earlier.

An airline which hit a lean patch following a series of airplane disasters hit upon the idea of promoting itself by offering their business customers free seats for their wives. In due time, the airline then wrote to the wives to ask how they had enjoyed their trip, hoping for some grateful and appreciative quotes that they could use in their publicity. In eighty-five per cent of the replies they received, however, the wives asked, 'Which trip?'

When a middle-aged gardener dis-covered that his wife had been unfaithful to him he took a novel form of revenge. Next time she left 'to visit her sister' he packed his lawnmower and all his possessions – except his watering can – into the family car.

He then sprinkled fast-growing lawn seed all over the carpets and soft furnishings, paying particular attention to the marital bed. He then watered the seed and locked up the house before driving off into the night. By the time his wife returned, the house was entirely covered in a light green growth of grass.

Maybe baby...?

A lawyer in America has said that he will leave his entire estate to the woman that gives birth to the most babies over a period of ten years.

A woman in Kansas tried to sue a pharmacy that sold her some contraceptive jelly. She claimed that the instructions were not clear, and that she fell pregnant despite having eaten the entire tube's contents on toast.

A pregnant woman in Manchester was accused of trying to shoplift a basketball.

A woman in Portugal decided that, after her fifth baby in as many years was born, that she had quite enough children and what she really needed was a car. She was arrested after advertising in a local paper to swap her latest, newborn child for a Ferrari.

Six babies were born at the same time on a cruise ship making its way back from New York: one in first class, two in second class, and three in third.

A baby born during a transatlantic flight to the US was awarded free travel for the rest of his life by the airline his mother was travelling on. This is rumoured to be standard practice for all airlines, which is perhaps partly why many restrict travel by expectant mothers!

Say Cheese!

A British couple with two young children decided to go on a camping holiday in France. They found a very pleasant campsite in Brittany and set up their large tent, looking forward to a quiet, relaxing time. However, to their dismay, the occupants of the tent next to theirs, a group of French twenty-somethings, turned out to be very loud, holding all-night parties and drinking heavily. The British family decided to complain to the management, who were very understanding and promised to ask the young revellers to leave immediately.

That night, by the time the family had returned from their day at the beach, their noisy neighbours had left. However, the family could tell that their tent had been broken into, for some of their personal belongings, like their toothbrushes, had been moved around. They reported the incident to the local police, but were not unduly worried as nothing had been stolen, and even their expensive new camera had been left behind.

They enjoyed the rest of their holiday until the time came to return to Britain. As soon as they got home, they developed their photographs from the trip, eager to have reminders of their lovely vacation. However, in amongst the standard snaps of the family on sightseeing jaunts and enjoying lavish meals, they were most surprised, and not at all pleased, to find several pictures of the noisy twenty-somethings in the family's tent, smiling delightedly, with each of the family's four toothbrushes up their bottoms!

That Sucks!

A British woman had an unexpected and rather embarrassing experience on her return flight from Europe. Barely half-an-hour into the flight, she accidentally flushed the toilet before getting up off it, and was unlucky enough to have her bottom sealed to the seat by the vacuum action of the suction toilet. It wasn't until the plane landed in London, over two hours later, that skilled technicians could come aboard and free her.

Classy Criminals

A man in Mexico was distraught when the expensive car he had bought just a week before was stolen from outside his house. Later that day he received a phone call from an anonymous man demanding eight thousand dollars as a ransom. The man paid the money and the next day he woke up to find his car, in perfect condition, parked outside his front door. There was a note under the windscreen wipers thanking him for the ransom money and promising that his car was now 'insured' for the next year.

However, the following week, the man again woke up to discover that the car had gone missing. Once again, that afternoon the man received the call asking for ransom money, whereupon the man complained that his car had supposedly been insured against theft. The anonymous caller quickly hung up. The next day when the man looked outside his front door it was to see his car parked outside with a bottle of champagne and a note of apology tucked into the wipers.

Do It Yourself
Next Time

A couple in Connecticut returned from holiday to find that their kitchen sink was blocked. Fancying himself to be reasonably handy around the house, the man offered to unblock it while his wife went out to do the grocery shopping. She left him with a spanner in his rubber-gloved hands.

It didn't take the man long to realize that the job was beyond him, and he therefore called his neighbour, a dab hand with DIY, to come around and help him fix it. The neighbour came around straightaway and got to work under the sink while the man went upstairs to begin unpacking his bags. When the woman returned from shopping, she saw the man's legs sticking out from under the sink and, believing it to be her husband, gave his bottom a playful smack. This, understandably, gave the helpful neighbour a bit of a shock, and he banged his head hard on the underside of the sink, knocking himself unconscious. The woman only realized her mistake when her husband came downstairs. They called for an ambulance, but the woes of the hapless neighbour were not yet over – the paramedics laughed so hard when they heard what had happened they dropped the stretcher and gave him another nasty bump!

Stag-gered!

A man about to get married was taken out to Blackpool on his stag night. Unsurprisingly, he got very drunk and ended up passing out in a nightclub. Some of his friends, who were medical students, decided, as was traditional, to play a trick on him. They took him to hospital and put both his legs, from toe to hip, in full plaster – so that he was plastered in both senses of the word!

The next morning, the young bridegroom woke up feeling distinctly worse for wear and most surprised to find both his legs encased in plaster. His friends explained that he had had a bad accident the night before – remembering little of it, the man believed them. He then had to suffer the inconvenience and embarrassment of hobbling down the aisle on crutches, not to mention the disapproval of his bride-to-be.

The friends allowed the poor bridegroom to go the whole of his wedding day struggling with his crutches, and to set off on his three-week honeymoon to Barbados still none the wiser that there was actually nothing wrong with his legs. They intended to call the hotel where the couple was staying to explain their trick, so as not to ruin the dream holiday. However, the couple, seeking complete privacy and seclusion, had deliberately left details of the wrong hotel and were therefore uncontactable. The pranksters had to wait until their friend returned from his holiday before they could make their rather red-faced apologies!

Unexpected Windfall

A gay man on a business trip in Scotland began chatting to a woman staying at his hotel. One thing led to another and they ended up spending the night together. The man did not want any complications to arise from the relationship, however, and gave her a false name – the name of his male partner back home.

When he returned home, he did not say anything to his partner about his unfaithfulness or about using his name. His partner was therefore very taken aback when, about a year on, he received a solicitor's letter telling him that a woman he had never heard of had died and left him all her money – a sizeable sum – and her thanks for that lovely night they had spent together!

Upwardly Mobile?

In the years before the use of mobile telephones became widespread, a young up and coming man in his twenties was on a train in London, speaking loudly into his, obviously proud of the status he believed it was lending him in the eyes of his fellow passengers.

At the same time, a few seats away, an elderly man became suddenly ill. The conductor was called but he explained that the train's communication system was broken and he therefore was unable to radio ahead to the next station to have an ambulance awaiting. A passenger sitting nearby pointed out that the solution was to ask the young man if they could borrow his phone. The conductor approached the man who was still in mid-conversation and, with an apology for interrupting, explained the emergency and asked to use the phone. The man ignored him and turned away. The conductor persisted, however, explaining how urgent the situation was, until eventually the young man, bright scarlet by this point, had to admit that the 'phone' was a fake and he had been using it purely as a prop!

Suspicious Minds

A pair of American research scientists working on a number of high-level, high-security projects were invited over to Russia for a conference. Before they went, their colleagues warned them that though the Cold War had long been over, it had still been known for the hotel rooms of American visitors to be bugged by the Russian government. Accordingly, when the two young scientists arrived and were shown to their luxurious hotel room in Moscow they immediately began to search the room for signs of a bug. Having checked the curtains, beds, light fittings and phone they had almost given up, when one of them spotted a tiny lump in the carpet in the middle of the room. They pulled up the carpet to take a closer look and found a small knob. Thinking their suspicions had been well-founded, they pulled out the knob. Just then, they heard a horrendous crash, the sound of splintering glass and the noise of voices raised in surprise – the knob they had pulled out had been holding up the huge glass chandelier in the function room below!

Give Us A Clue

An army officer was invited to a very smart dinner at a friend's house. When he sat down to dinner, he noticed that the woman sitting next to him seemed very familiar. He was very sure that he knew her, but, not wanting to confess that he had forgotten her name, he asked her how her brother was getting along, hoping that her reply would provide some clue as to her identity. However, she replied politely that she did not have a brother. Noticing the wedding ring on her left hand and wondering if he perhaps knew through her spouse, he then asked her how her husband was and whether he was still in the same job. The woman stared at him for a moment before replying. 'He's fine,' she said with a grin. 'Still President.'

Apology Excepted

An airline based in a particularly cockroach-infested region of South Africa frequently had problems with the insects getting into the planes and into the luggage of the passengers. One man was so disgusted to find a cockroach in the dessert of the meal he had been served aboard one of the planes that he wrote a long and very stern letter of complaint.

A few weeks later, the airline sent him a grovelling letter in return, apologizing profusely for the incident and explaining it was not the fault of the airline, but of the airport staff and the local government. Nevertheless, the letter told of the airline's horror and sympathy that it should have happened and offered him an upgrade to first class next time he travelled with them. Somewhat mollified, the man filed the letter and went to throw the envelope away. As he did so, he spotted a scrap of paper in there and took it out to read. The note, obviously written for the guidance of a secretary or administrator, read 'Another loser whingeing about the roaches. Just send him the standard letter.'

Teed Off!

A businessman who prided himself on his golfing abilities was glad of the opportunity to show off his skills to an important client who was visiting from Hamburg. That day was not one of his better days, however, and after several bad shots during which he lost balls in the rough and in the lake, his temper got the better of him. Much to the astonishment of his foreign visitor, he grabbed his golf bag, full of his clubs, and hurled it as hard as he could into the lake, before storming off. Barely a minute later, he realized, to his dismay, that the bag had contained his car keys and was forced, in front of his amazed client, to wade into the lake to retrieve the bag.

Celebrity Snub

Several years ago, a young ambitious city worker named Robert Harris was out on a business lunch with his boss when he spotted Frank Sinatra on the other side of the restaurant. Excusing himself from the table, he went over to the singer and, after introducing himself and complimenting him on his recent work, he went on to ask a favour. He explained that he was having lunch with his boss to discuss the possibility of his promotion and, as the boss was a huge fan of Frank's, that it would help his cause no end if the celebrity singer would come over to their table and pretend to know the young man.

Very kindly, the singer agreed and the man returned to his table. A few moments later, Frank Sinatra came over to the young man's table as requested and, putting a friendly hand on his shoulder, said, 'Hey, Bob, haven't seen you for a while. How's it going?' To which the young man rudely replied, 'Get lost, Frank. Can't you see I'm in the middle of a meeting?'

Royal Lunatic

A head chef named Franco who worked in one of Spain's most prestigious restaurants was delighted when he was honoured with a request from the King of Spain to cook a three course meal for a delegation of important foreign visitors. He spent three weeks planning the menu and preparing for the dinner, and, by the time the day of the event arrived, he was very excited and nervous. He took his own knives, as was his tradition, and it being rush hour, had quite a job to catch a taxi. Eventually, he flagged one down and told the driver to hurry to the Palace as he had to meet the King. The driver looked surprised but drove on. The chef sat in the back of the cab, nervously checking his bag of knives to make sure he hadn't forgotten anything and muttering to himself the menu he was planning.

By this stage, the taxi driver was convinced that the man was insane and, taking it upon himself to save the King from this madman with his collection of knives, drove him instead to the mental hospital. When the cab arrived, the chef, not noticing in his nervous state that this was not the Palace, leapt out and declared to the doorman that he was Franco and he wanted to see the King. Spotting his collection of knives, staff promptly grabbed him and admitted him to the hospital. Despite his protests when he finally realized where he was, he was held there for several hours until rescued by his colleagues. Unfortunately for him, he was not in time to get to the Palace and make his lavish meal.

Weather
or not
You
Believe
It...

Pennies From Heaven?

In a town in Guatemala, money, blue rain, frogs and toads, fish, gold, cigarettes and Star Wars figures have on separate occasions rained from the sky.

An impoverished Romanian woman was at first most upset to be struck very hard on the head by a large hailstone during a storm. She soon forgot the pain, however, when she found a diamond ring inside it.

The corners that are cut off green Rizlas (rolling papers) are used to make fake snow in low-budget movies.

A poor village in Mexico was showered with gold from the sky. Supposedly a treasure chest from a ship sunk off the nearby coast was whipped up by a tornado and deposited on the village.

A boy in Africa was hit on the head and knocked out by a pebble-sized meteorite. When scientists examined the meteorite, they discovered that it had been travelling through space for billions of years – only to fly into the head of a small Earth boy!

In many villages in southern Ukraine, farmers believe that when pigs pick up their straw and carry it back to their sties, it means a bad storm is on its way.

Seeing The Light...

A man in Holland who was extremely depressed as he believed his wife was about to leave him because he had become impotent, decided he would end it all rather than live without her. He climbed a tree in a nearby field in order to hang himself. Suddenly, just as he was attaching the rope to the tree, a bolt of lighting struck him in the groin. He was found a couple of hours later lying beside the tree unconscious and was rushed to hospital. At first disappointed that his suicide attempt was so unsuccessful, he soon cheered up no end when, almost immediately after he left hospital, he found that he could make love to his wife again.

A middle-aged man was arrested in Iowa for running along the interstate with no clothes on during a very heavy storm. He had been running for quite some time and several motorists had called in to report his strange apperarance. When the police finally caught up with him and asked what he was doing he replied, 'The lightning told me to undress and run as fast as I could.'

A man in Texas was being readied to die by electric chair for murdering three people. As he was brought to the chair, he screamed out, 'I'm innocent!'. At that moment, a surge of electricity struck the chair burning it to the ground. The execution was postponed and two days later the real killer confessed.

Head In The Clouds?

During World War II a British bomber was shot down over Germany. Three of the crew managed to jump from the burning plane in time, but did not have a chance to actually put their parachutes on, they had to leap just holding on to them. Amazingly they landed on a cloud and fell no further. They were held up in the cloud by the hailstones and rain brewing in its mass. The three men had time to put on their chutes properly before they continued their descent. They all landed safely.

Spinning A Good Yarn...

A tornado in South Dakota swept up a passenger train, spun it around in mid air, and placed it back on the tracks facing in the opposite direction.

During Hurricane Gilbert a couple's house was all but levelled by the devastating storm. Even more distressing was the fact that their young baby was picked up in its cradle and carried away by the strong winds. After hours of frantic searching, without holding out much hope for the baby's survival, they were both relieved and astounded to find that it had landed safely in an apple tree over two miles away.

A team of archaeologists working on a lost city in Borneo were warned to take shelter from an impending hurricane. The hurricane came through that night and when the team re-emerged in the morning they discovered that virtually the whole city had been unearthed. This kind of excavation would have taken a year with manpower alone.

Police were called to a launderette in Nashville when a man walked in from a rainstorm, put a few coins in a machine, climbed in and began to tumble dry himself.

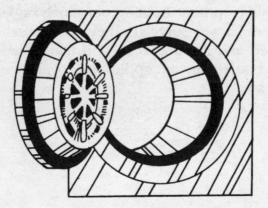

On Your Bike!

In September 1994, a previously un-successful campaigner and ex-stand-up comedian, Jacob Hauguard, managed to get elected into the Danish parliament after promising better tail winds for cyclists.

Dressing It Up...

A childish prank left a man in prison for eight months after he held a magnifying glass to the back of a friend's dress in the middle of a heatwave. The dress caught fire, causing the woman third-degree burns.

It's A Steal

A thief who stole the contents of the collection plate in a Moldovan church was pinned to a pew by a large icicle as he tried to make his escape. It was so cold in the church that icicles had formed where there were leaks in the roof.

It's A Sign...

At the very same moment that Stalin was signing a treaty with Hitler, the skies over Bergof, Hitler's private retreat, turned blood red.

I'll Be Blowed...

A garden ornament maker in Ecuador was working in his yard when his house was struck by a passing hurricane. He grabbed his video camera to record the amazing noise and destruction that the storm was making. As well as videoing the neighbouring roofs being blown off and trees being upended, the man also recorded the huge swell of noise made when the wind caught his array of wind chimes. While the hurricane was exciting enough, there was another unexpected shock to come: when the man played the video back later that same day he could distinctly hear the first four bars of Mozart's requiem, with harmonies and accompaniments, being played on his chimes as the wind whistled past.

A Load Of Old Balls...

A small boy was playing in the freshly-fallen snow outside his home in the Czech republic. After having made a snowman, the child then made several snowballs and began throwing them on to the sloping roof of a factory in Czechoslovakia. Just then, one of the large bears who were known to live in the nearby woods appeared and started to run towards the boy. Thinking he was done for, the boy began to scream in terror. Luckily, however, as the bear reared up to attack, the boy's scream was loud enough to dislodge one of the snowballs that he had thrown earlier. It rolled back down the roof – only twenty times its original size. It hit the bear hard on the head, scaring it away.

All Michael O'Mara titles are available by post from:
Bookpost, P.O. Box 29, Douglas, Isle of Man IM99 1BQ

Credit cards accepted.
Please telephone 01624 836000
Fax 01624 837033
Internet http://www.bookpost.co.uk

Free postage and packing in the UK.
Overseas customers allow £1 per book (paperbacks)
And £3.00 per book (hardbacks)

Other humour titles:
The World's Stupidest Criminals – ISBN 1-85479-879-0
The World's Stupidest Graffiti – ISBN – 1-85479-876-6
The World's Stupidest Men – ISBN – 1-85479-508-2
The World's Stupidest Laws – ISBN 1-85479-549-X
The World's Stupidest Signs – ISBN 1-85479-555-4
Outrageous Expressions – ISBN 1-85479-556-2
Totally Stupid Men – ISBN 1-85479-274-1
Stupid Men Quiz Book – ISBN 1-85479-693-3
Complete Crap – ISBN 1-85479-313-6
Wicked Cockney Rhyming Slang –ISBN 1-85479-386-1
All Men Are Bastards – ISBN 1-85479-387-X
The Ultimate Book of Farting – ISBN 1-85479-596-1
The Complete Book of Farting – ISBN 1-85479-440-X
The History of Farting –ISBN 1-85479-754-9
The Ultimate Insult – ISBN 1-85479-288-1
The Little Englander's Handbook – 1-85479-553-8